The First Chester Book of Motets

The Italian School for 4 voices

Edited by Anthony G. Petti

LIST OF MOTETS

CHESTER MUSIC
J. & W. Chester/Edition Wilhelm Hansen London Ltd.

INTRODUCTION

While the madrigal is now coming into its own in terms of individual editions and collections, the motet is sti
somewhat neglected, and has even suffered a setback, because the disappearance of Latin from the Roman Cathol
liturgy has caused many works to go out of print. Musicologists continue to introduce new editions, but their ma
emphasis is on the provision of larger scale works for the concert hall or of scholarly editions which are often beyon
the scope of the average choir to decipher and transpose, let alone sing.

The aim of the present series is to make more readily available a comprehensive body of Latin motets from th
Renaissance period, combining old favourites with lesser known or hitherto unpublished works. The first five volumes a
arranged nationally, covering Italy, the Low Countries, Spain, Germany and Slavic areas, and England, and each co
tains, on average, twelve motets drawn from not less than six composers. They are for four mixed voices, and shou
all be within the scope of the reasonably able choir. They also provide a fair selection from the liturgical year, as
guide for the church choir and for performing choirs who like to present their music according to theme or seaso

The editor has endeavoured to preserve a balance between a critical and a performing edition. The motets are tran
posed into the most practical performing keys, are barred, fully underlayed, provided with breathing marks, and have
reduction as a rehearsal aid. Editorial tempi and dynamics are also supplied, but only in the reduction, leaving cho
masters free to select their own in the light of their interpretation of a given piece, vocal resources and the acoustic
The vocal range for all parts is given at the beginning of each motet.

As an aid to musicologists, the motets, wherever possible, are transcribed from the most authoritative source, ar
the original clefs, signatures and note values are given at the beginning and wherever they change during the course of
piece. Ligatures are indicated by slurs, editorial accidentals are placed above the stave, and the underlay is shown
italics when it expands a ditto sign, or in square brackets when entirely editorial.

Each volume includes a brief introduction concerning the scope of the edition, with notes on the composers, th
motets, the sources, editorial emendations and alterations, if any, and a table of use according to the Tridentine Rit

The main concentration in this volume is on the late 16th century, because it is the best period of Italian pol
phony, but four works from the early 17th century are included as showing an interesting transition from the Hig
Renaissance to the Early Baroque. Understandably, Palestrina is strongly represented because he dominated the Roma
School. Marenzio has also been accorded more than one motet on the grounds that his sacred music tends to be ove
shadowed by his madrigals.

The first two composers represented here are the Anerio brothers, Felice (1560-1614) and Giovanni Francesc
(1567-1630), who came from a very musical family and began their careers as boy sopranos, both singing for a tim
under Palestrina. Felice eventually succeeded Palestrina as composer to the Papal Chapel. Though he is celebrated fo
his influential part-songs, his achievement in church music is also considerable, including two volumes of sacred hym
for five, six, seven and eight voices (1596, 1602), and a set of Tenebrae Responsories (1606), which, though influenc
in places by Victoria's settings, are nevertheless generally original, and have a strongly emotive but aesthetically co
trolled appeal. Ironically, the work for which he is best known, the *Christus Factus Est* does not appear to have bee
published in his lifetime, and it was certainly not printed with the Tenebrae Responsories as some have suggested.
manuscript copy of it was apparently housed in the Collegio Romano, but this seems to have vanished not long aft
it was transcribed by Alfieri in his *Raccolta di Mottetti a Quattro Voci di Palestrina, di Vittoria, e di Felice Aneri*
(1840), a collection to which modern editors of this motet are directly or indirectly indebted. Among the notable featur
of *Christus Factus Est* is the innovation of beginning with an exposed dissonanace of a close second, with the al
starting above the cantus, followed by a similar dissonance only one beat after the resolution of the first. Also to
noted are the subtle modulations of 'usque ad mortem", the change from duple to triple time and back again — unusu
in so short a piece — and the bass leap of a minor sixth on "obediens", all of which are suggestive of the Early Baroqu
style. There are also problems of *musica ficta*, though the general style seems to require F♯ in bars 2-5 but probably n
in bar 1.

Giovanni Francesco Anerio held several musical directorships in Italy, including that of Santa Maria dei Mon
(1613-21), and in later life became *maestro di cappella* at the Polish Court of Sigismund III. He was a more prolif
composer than Felice, with volumes of motets and spiritual madrigals (1609, 1611, 1613, 1618), litanies (1611
masses (1614), and vesper psalms (1620). His *Teatro Armónico Spirituale* (1619), with its dramatic *lauda* settings ar
use of *basso continuo* is markedly in the Early Baroque tradition and makes an important contribution to the foundi
of oratorio. The *Requiem Aeternam* included here forms the Introit of his *Missa pro Defunctis*, first published in h
collection of masses in 1614 and subsequently issued separately in three further editions in the 17th century. Like th
rest of the Mass, the Introit perfectly blends traditional and new elements to form a setting both tender and stirrin
Plainsong figures prominently, providing the intonations for the antiphon and the psalm verse and the *cantus firmus*
the tenor in the first part of the antiphon. A slow delicate fugue is used to convey the supplicatory mood of the antipho
an exultant homophonic declamation takes over the "Et tibi reddetur", but is succeeded by a "mixed" style for th
gently descending cadences of "ad te omnis caro veniet".

While the Anerio brothers can be described as of the Roman School, the third composer in this volume, Giovan
Croce (1557-1607), a pupil of Zarlino, was a Venetian through and through, spending virtually all his musical life
St. Mark's, which he entered as a singer at the age of eight, eventually becoming *maestro di cappella* on the death
Donati in 1603. As might be expected of a member of the Venetian School, most of Croce's considerable corpus
sacred music is polychoral, including several books of motets and psalms for eight voices (1591, 1594, 1595, 159

1597), some intended for accompaniment with diverse instruments (1594, 1610). The style is often elaborately contrapuntal as well as polychoral, but that Croce was capable of writing in a simple and unobtrusively mellifluous way is indicated by his four-part collection, *Motetti a Quattro Voci* (1597), from which *O Sacrum Convivium* is taken. This motet seems to show affinities with the Roman School, though its polyphony is chastened, its harmonies are quite close, and it has one or two swift-moving figures (cantus, bar 10) and touches of syncopation (tenor, bar 21) which help to distinguish it. One of its most pleasing as well as distinctive features is its repeated coda for "alleluia", which begins in homophonic, marcato style in pairs of voices, and then fans out into patterns of melisma.

Croce is a somewhat neglected composer, and the same could be said of Marc Antonio Ingegneri (c. 1545-92). A native of Verona (but of a Venetian family which was credited with the invention of the pneumatic organ), he studied at Verona Cathedral under Ruffo and probably Asola as well. He moved to Cremona in 1568, and in time became *maestro di cappella* at the cathedral, the young Monteverdi being among his pupils. In addition to being an able musical director, Ingegneri was a fine singer, organist and string player. He published several volumes of masses and motets, mainly for five voices (1573, 1576, 1586, 1587), and also wrote polychoral music for as many as sixteen voices accompanied by instruments (*Liber Sacrarum Cantionum*, 1589). However, he composed at least two volumes of four-part motets, one of which was the *Responsoria Hebdomadae Sanctae* (with six-part *Miserere*), 1588, from which *In Monte Oliveti* is taken. This set of Responsories was ascribed to Palestrina by no less a musicologist than Haberl, who transcribed them from a manuscript source in his complete works of Palestrina shortly before the 1588 edition was discovered in 1897. Ingegneri, like Felice Anerio and Croce, was one of many who set the Tenebrae Responsories, understandably so, because of the poignancy of the texts. He, too, seems to have been influenced by Victoria's settings (published in 1585), and, in turn, apparently influenced Croce (compare, for example, their two versions of *In Monte Oliveti*). Ingegneri's settings are very compact, with very little verbal repetition, yet maintaining an incredible smoothness and beauty of melodic line. They keep very closely to the speech rhythms and verbal accentuation, and use a fair amount of word-painting. Especially to be noted in the present piece is the slow ascending passage for depicting the Mount of Olives (bars 1-6), the homophonic cry on "Pater", the very exposed ascent of the top line for "transeat a me" (bars 13-14), the suspension on "infirma" (bar 25), and the pained resignation reinforced by the A♭ chord towards the end of the main section (bar 28). Ingegneri has followed Victoria's general practice of setting the versicle as a trio, and has lightened the effect still further by splitting the cantus line in what is one of the loveliest pieces of three-part writing in 16th century polyphony.

Luca Marenzio (c. 1553-99) is the only one of the group represented here whose secular music is more copious than his sacred music, though he too had to find church employment to earn a living. He began as a boy singer at the cathedral of his native city of Brescia, studied under Contini, and rose to the post of organist. He moved soon after to Rome, where he became choirmaster to the powerful Cardinal d'Este, and was later patronized by Cardinal Aldobrandini. He travelled considerably, going to Florence and, like Giovanni Francesco Anerio after him, to the court of Sigismund III of Poland. In his final years he was attached to the Papal Chapel. Apart from publishing nine books of madrigals, Marenzio composed a considerable amount of sacred music, though the surviving works are limited mainly to *Sacrae Cantiones* (written in his youth but extant only in the 1616 edition), and *Montecta Festorum Totius Anni* (1585), from which the present two examples are taken. Both motets show strong madrigalian influence and contain much word-painting. The most obvious instances in *O Rex Gloriae* are paired ascending scale passages for "super omnes caelos ascendisti" (bars 25-30) and corresponding scale duets for the descent of the Holy Spirit, "Spiritum veritatis" (bars 39-43). The motet also includes very breezy, highly rhythmic and swift-moving phrases for "qui triumphator" (bars 40-2), and ends with a mainly homophonic section of unusually angular and jaunty alleluias which include the rare drop of a diminished fifth (tenor, bars 49-50). The *Tribus Miraculis* is more in Church style, but it too has secular features, with its intricate and florid writing (e.g., in the opening), the descriptive star-led train for "stella Magos" (bars 13-18), and the triumphant quasi-madrigalian conclusion. Both motets use a homophonic technique for each "hodie", not only to solemnize the announcement but also seemingly to make it a rendezvous point before the parts move off again on their frequently exposed and syncopated way.

In making selections from Palestrina (c. 1525-94) one has an embarrassment of choice, for he is one of the most prolific of Renaissance composers, and maintains a generally high standard, even if he nods occasionally in his collection of ninety four masses. There are over one hundred four-part hymns and motets to choose from, but probably the most fruitful source is the *Motettorum Quattuor Vocibua, Liber Secundus*, first published in Venice in 1581, and reprinted several times. It is from this collection that three of the motets have been selected: *Ego Sum Panis Vivus, Sicut Cervus*, and *Super Flumina*. Of these, *Ego Sum* seems the least mature work, for it has not quite the grace and smoothness of the others, and is a little more difficult to sing well than is usual for the best of Palestrina. Nevertheless, it contains many haunting phrases and much melismatic sweetness. Above all, it has a fine sense of structure, falling into two well-balanced sections, each beginning with a high-lying and well developed fugue, the first coming to rest on an appropriately low cadence for "mortui sunt" (bars 30-4), the second, with its climactic repetition of "non morietur", ending with a strong affirmation of faith through music. *Sicut Cervus*, the first part of a double motet (the second part being the equally impressive *Sitivit Anima Mea*) has a delicate beauty, its gently flowing and dovetailing phrases being filled with a joyful tranquillity which suddenly gains intensity and a sense of yearning with the approach of the cross-rhythms of "anima mea". It ends with a "step and leap" movement in each voice as it aspires to reach God in "ad te, Deus". *Super Flumina* seems to be the quintessential musical expression of grief in exile, gradually building up momentum from the opening melisma of sorrow to the release of pent-up anguish in "suspendimus organo". The motet ends in a tortured irresolute Phrygian cadence in an otherwise Aeolian motet. By contrast with these three works, the *Alma Redemptoris* is very compact and remarkably brief, though without the slightest sense of haste or incompleteness. It is mainly homophonic, but with touches of the polyphonic style for key words like "Virgo" (Bars 23-6) and, more especially, "peccatorum", where it contributes to the fine sense of climax which Palestrina always seems to achieve more effectively than most of his contemporaries. This motet indicates how skilfully Palestrina employs plainsong, for he not only uses the simple chant *Alma Redemptoris* for the intonation but embeds it so well in the main fabric of the music that it seems to form a new whole. Like Felice Anerio's *Christus Factus Est*, this great yet simple work was not published in the composer's lifetime, and the manuscript copy of it from which Alfieri prepared a transcription for the *Raccolta* of 1840 was apparently lost when the library of the Collegio Romano was dispersed in the late 19th century.

Among Palestrina's most distinguished pupils was Francesco Soriano (1549-1621). He was a choir-boy at St. John Lateran in Rome, became choirmaster at the church of St. Louis of France, and then, on the recommendation of Palestrina, went to the court at Mantua. Towards the end of the century he was successively director of music at some of the most important churches in Rome, including Santa Maria Maggiore, and in 1603 obtained the prized position of director of the Cappella Giulia, retaining the post until his death. Among Soriano's diverse works are volumes of poly-choral masses and motets (1609, 1616) and a remarkably mixed collection of pieces, containing a Passion, a Magnificat for sixteen voices, and a Sequence and Responsory for the Dead for four voices, published in Rome in 1619. This work also includes antiphones to the Blessed Virgin, one of which, the *Regina Caeli*, is published here. Though Soriano is usually noted for the Early Baroque features of the use of soloists, chromaticism, and the provision of a *basso continuo*, the *Regina Caeli* is characterised by simplicity, a reliance on the simple chant of the antiphon for the framework of the melodic line, and on fairly traditional and unobtrusive harmonies. One of the strengths of the piece is the way in which the music acts as a handmaiden to the words rather than trying to dominate them.

Ludovico da Viadana, more properly known as Ludovico Grossi (c. 1564-1645), was a pupil of Costanzo Porta. His most important musical appointments were as *maestro di cappella* at Mantua Cathedral (before 1590), at Concordia in 1609, and at Fano Cathedral in 1612. He became a Franciscan in 1609, and retired to the monastery of Gualtieri for about the last twenty five years of his life. His compositions include masses and psalms, but he is best remembered for his *Cento Concerti Ecclesiastici*, first published in 1602. This comprises one hundred motets and psalm settings for from one to four voices, with organ continuo. Though the work contained supposed innovations by providing solo works and organ accompaniment, these features had been in existence for some time. The general standard of the collection is high and there is a conserable variety of mood and style. The *Exsultate Justi*, which comes from this work is the only one of the motets published here for which organ accompaniment was definitely intended (though it is not strictly necessary). It is a remarkably lively piece with well-sustained momentum, with an ABA form alternating fast triple and duple times. The style is mainly homophonic, with some fugal writing in the middle section. Note values are wide-ranging, with a profusion of short notes set monosyllabically, a style becoming quite popular in the period. The most notable feature of the motet is its onomatopoeic representation of musical instruments and sounds, with the arpeggio-like passages for "cithara" (bar 19), the long quasi-solo run for "novum" (bars 38-9), and the percussive "vociferatione" (bars 55-62). It is a fittingly exuberant piece with which to conclude an anthology.

Anthony G. Petti. 1977

Table of use according to the Tridentine Rite

Motet	liturgical source	seasonal and festal use
Christus Factus Est	Gradual for Maundy Thursday	Lent, Passiontide, General
Requiem Aeternam	Introit, Mass for the Dead	All Souls, Funerals
O Sacrum Convivium	*Magnificat* ant., 2nd Vespers, Corpus Christi	Corpus Christi, Communion, except in Lent
In Monte Oliveti	Resp., 1st Nocturn, Matins, Maunday Thursday	Lent, Passiontide
O Rex Gloriae	*Magnificat* ant., 2nd Vespers, Ascension Day	Ascension
Tribus Miraculis	*Magnificat* ant., 2nd Vespers, Epiphany	Epiphany to Septuagesima
Alma Redemptoris	Ant. of the Blessed Virgin, Advent to Purification	Advent to Purification,
Ego Sum Panis Vivus	*Benedictus* ant., Lauds, Corpus Christi	Corpus Christi, Communion
Sicut Cervus	Tract, Procession to Fount, Holy Saturday	Holy Saturday, General
Super Flumina	Offertory, 20th Sunday after Pentecost	20th Sunday after Pentecost, Lent, General
Regina Caeli	Ant. of the Blessed Virgin, Easter to Pentecost	Easter
Exsultate Justi	Ant. and psalm, None	General

CHRISTUS FACTUS EST

Christ was made obedient even to death, death on the cross. God therefore
exalted him and gave him a name excelling all others.

(*Philippians*, ii, 8-9)

Felice Anerio
(1560 - 1614)

3

REQUIEM AETERNAM

(Introit : Mass for the Dead)

Grant them eternal rest, O Lord, and let perpetual light shine on them.
Ps. To you we owe a hymn in Sion, and the vow made to you shall be kept in
Jerusalem. Hear my prayer: all flesh must come to you.

(4 *Esdras,* i i, 34-5 ; *Ps.* lxiv, 2-3.)

Giovanni Francesco Aner
(1567 - 1630)

Requiem aeternam *ut supra.*

O SACRUM CONVIVIUM

O sacred banquet, in which Christ is received, the memory of his passion renewed,
the mind filled with grace, and a promise of future glory given to us.
Alleluia.

Giovanni Croce
(1557 - 1607)

IN MONTE OLIVETI

On the Mount of Olives he prayed to his father: Father, if it be possible,
let this chalice pass from me. The spirit is willing, but the flesh is weak:
your will be done. Watch and pray lest you enter into temptation.
(*Matthew*, xxvi, 39, 41)

Marc Antonio Ingegne
(1545 - 1592)

11

12

§ Spiritus quidem *ut supr*

O REX GLORIAE

O King of Glory, Lord of Hosts, who have this day ascended in triumph above
all the heavens: do not leave us orphans, but send us the Promise of the Father,
the Spirit of Truth. Alleluia.   (*Ps.* xxiii, 10; *Eph.*. iv, 10; *John,* xiv, 18; *Luke* xxiv, 49.)

Luca Marenzio
(1553 - 1599)

TRIBUS MIRACULIS

We celebrate a day sanctified by three miracles: today a star led the Wise
Men to the manger; today water was changed into wine at the marriage
feast; today Christ chose to be baptised by John in the Jordan for our salvation.
Alleluia.

Luca Marenzio
(1553 - 1599)

18

ALMA REDEMPTORIS

Kind mother of the Redeemer, the open gateway to heaven and star of the sea,
help your fallen people who strive to rise again: we pray you, who bore your holy Son
by a miracle of nature, a virgin first and last, who received God's greeting from
the mouth of Gabriel, have mercy on sinners.

(attrib. Hermann Contractus.)

G. P. da Palestrina
(1525 - 1594)

EGO SUM PANIS VIVUS

I am the living bread. Your forefathers ate manna in the desert and are dead;
this is living bread from heaven: whoever eats it shall not die.

(*John,* vi.)

G. P. da Palestrina
(1525 - 1594)

SICUT CERVUS

As the hart longs for water, so my soul yearns for you, O God.

(*Ps. xli*, 2.)

G. P. da Palestrina
(1525 - 1594)

30

SUPER FLUMINA

By the waters of Babylon we sat down and wept when we remembered you,
Sion: on the willow trees which grow in their midst did we hang our harps.
(*Ps. cxxxvi,* **1.**)

G. P. da Palestrina
(1525 - 1594)

32

REGINA CAELI

Queen of heaven, be joyful, alleluia; for he whom you were worthy to bear,
alleluia, has risen as he promised, alleluia.
Pray for us to God, alleluia.

Francesco Soriano
(1549 - 1621)

36

EXSULTATE JUSTI

Let the just rejoice in the Lord: it is fitting for the upright to praise him.
Sing to him to the psaltery and the ten-stringed lute. Make him a new song:
sing to him well with strong voice. (*Ps. xxxii*, **1-2.**)

Ludovico da Viadana
(1564 - 1645)